Lochaber
and the Road to the Isles

compiled by

Christopher J. Uncles

Royalties arising from the sale of the first edition of this book will be donated to the West Highland Museum, Fort William.

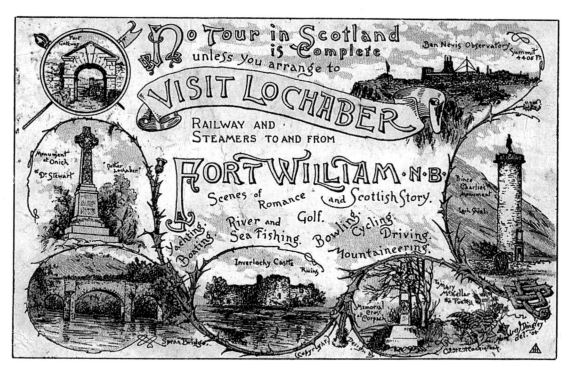

The attractions of Lochaber as advertised c1900.

Richard Stenlake Publishing
1996

ACKNOWLEDGEMENTS

My sincere thanks are given to those who kindly responded with help to often
obscure queries, and for permitting photographs to be reproduced:

Sir Donald H. Cameron of Lochiel KT; Diana and Barrie Gent; Ronnie MacKellaig;
Mr and Mrs E.D. MacMillan; Fiona Marwick; The Northern Lighthouse Board;
Ruth and John Smither; Alastair J.B. White. I am especially grateful to
Mrs Susan Girling who permitted reproduction of material relating to her
grandfather, the late C.D. Rudd of Ardnamurchan, and for providing access to
A Compendium of his Life written by her father Alan Rudd, and published privately.
Lastly, and by no means least, to my wife, Angela, who prepared the manuscript,
and without whose help, interest and encouragement, it would probably have
never seen the light of day.

A few anonymously published postcards appear in the book; the publishers will
be pleased to entertain acknowledgements in these cases for future editions.

Arisaig Station, showing the Sgurr of Eigg on the horizon, c1902.

INTRODUCTION

Lochaber may be broadly defined as all that part of the Scottish mainland lying to the west of a line drawn from Invergarry, around Loch Ossian and Glen Coe to Keil on Loch Linnhe - and including the adjacent islands of Canna, Rum, Eigg and Muck. Formerly administered by both Inverness-shire and Argyll, Lochaber is now part of Highland region. Its economic and social centre is Fort William.

There are several outstanding natural features within the Lochaber boundaries, including Ben Nevis, Loch Morar and Ardnamurchan Point; Britain's highest mountain, deepest freshwater loch, and most westerly mainland point respectively. The area is also rich in historical and industrial associations. These range from memories of Bonnie Prince Charlie and the '45, to Telford's great Caledonian Canal, and the landmark development at Kinlochleven. Add to these the magic of 'The Road to the Isles', and the excitement of taking one of The Great Train Journeys of the World over the desolate Moor of Rannoch to Fort William and Mallaig, and the variety of Lochaber's attractions is as wide as one could wish.

Much has been written about this land of mountain and loch, sometimes by writers who knew it so intimately that they almost believed parts of it to be their own personal preserve. One such person was the redoubtable Miss Mary Ethel Muir Donaldson (1876-1958), scholar, author and photographer, who built her own house in Ardnamurchan of local materials and to exacting specifications. A fervent Jacobite, she deplored alien development, and in particular what she saw as human intrusion into northern Lochaber, Prince Charlie's country. Writing in the 1920s, she described the Glenfinnan monument as 'a fifth rate lighthouse', and Sir Robert McAlpine's nearby viaduct as 'vile'. Fort William was 'an ugly little town compacted of hideous buildings', and in Mallaig she found 'aggressive buildings incongruous in their setting'. Neither did Glenborrodale Castle nor Arisaig House fare any better.

But 'we are of our time'. Miss Donaldson was in her mid-twenties at the turn of the century when the West Highland Railway was under construction, pushing westwards through virgin territory to Mallaig, and it is easy enough to understand how many must have viewed what they saw as the despoilation of the lonely, wild and empty glens.

The coming of the railway in 1894 was the spur to Fort William's development, and prior to its arrival there in 1901 Mallaig was virtually non-existent. Both are now busy working towns, each with a distinct character, although it has to be admitted that town planners have not always served them well.

Photographs are perhaps the most valuable record of the past, better by far than the most descriptive prose or the fallible memory of old age, and I hope that this collection of pictures will evoke more than mere nostalgia. Most of these photographs were taken in the early days of photography, before the First World War. They required the use of weighty tripods, bulky cameras, and heavy glass plate negatives, and a great debt is due to the unknown photographers behind this collection, who have left us a marvellous legacy to study and enjoy.

For all those who enjoyed *Last Ferry To Skye*, I hope that this companion volume will give as much pleasure. The photographs have been arranged in four sections: Fort William and Ben Nevis; Lochaber: Here and There; The Road to Ardnamurchan; and The Road to the Isles.

Christopher J. Uncles

The *Maid of Glencoe* with two cars aboard is being secured at
the jetty of the Loch Leven ferry crossing during the 1930s.

FORT WILLIAM AND BEN NEVIS

The settlement on the eastern shore of Loch Linnhe that eventually grew to become the town of Fort William originated in Cromwellian times. Acting on instructions from London, General Monk established a turf fortification there in the 1650s. This served as a base for troops from which unruly clans, especially the Camerons, could be subjugated, and in the reign of William III the fort was rebuilt of stone and the Jacobite attacks of 1745 subsequently repulsed. Although known for short periods as Maryburgh, Gordonsburgh and Duncansburgh, the name Fort William remained. At the turn of the 20th century its population amounted to 2,000 inhabitants.

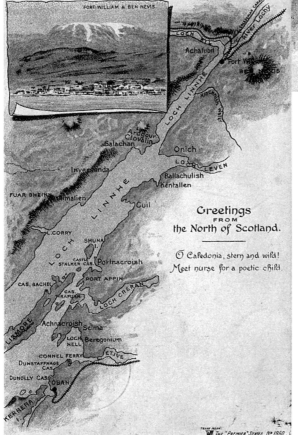

These two early Edwardian postcards show the situation of the town in relation to both Inverness (the Highland capital) and Oban. Located at the hub of land routes up and down the Great Glen (which also carries the Caledonian Canal), Fort William has always been a place of strategic importance. The wild lands of Badenoch lie eastwards beyond Glen Spean, while Arisaig and the islands of the west are accessible beyond the northern shore of Loch Eil.

Despite the presence of some substantial Victorian villas along the Achintore road (Fort William's 'West End'), the tilled fields and bare hillsides give this 1892 photograph a distinctly rural atmosphere. Some difference today!

Achintore Road, photographed during the 1890s, with people relaxing on the verges and strolling along the lochside. Note the ornamental lampstandards. In 1894, the Fort William Electric Lighting Company established Fort William as the first town in Britain to have its streets lit by locally produced electricity.

Situated on a prestigious site overlooking both the town and loch, the Station Hotel is a fine building, incorporating ornamental ironwork and decorative woodwork to soften the sharpness of the elevations. The man caught on a window ledge by the photographer in this 1896 picture is not a guest leaving surreptitiously without paying his bill, but a window cleaner!

A postcard advertisement for the Station Hotel, c1900.

This turn of the century picture emphasises the size of the Station Hotel (later Highland Hotel) in relation to existing buildings, and illustrates its position in the growing tiered development taking place on the hillside above the town.

A group of children on Union Road where it joins Lundavara Road. This perspective of the Station Hotel has become obscured by residential development since the late nineteenth century, when this photograph was taken.

Above: Fort William photographed from the Treslaig shore, 1892.   The High Street had already been formed by this time, and the town's linear development along the lochside is clearly apparent here. Several fine buildings are in evidence, including St Andrew's Church, whose spire is visible on the left. Gordon Square, a place of considerable activity when steamers arrived and departed, lies behind the paddle steamer at the pier.   The bulky outline of Ben Nevis, Britain's highest mountain (4406 feet above sea level) and twenty-four miles in circumference, dominates the whole area.

Below: Compare this 1895 photograph with its counterpart taken three years earlier. A retaining sea wall has been built along Loch Linnhe to protect the newly built railway line, and the twin platform canopies are visible right of centre at the station terminus (which adjoins Gordon Square pierhead). Immediately behind on the hillside above, a large site is being cleared for what will become one of the Fort's best known landmarks, the Station Hotel.

Upper Achintore has been much changed by development since this photograph was taken in 1931.

In 1890, a low level observatory was built at Achintore to complement the mountain observatory which had been established on Ben Nevis summit seven years earlier. Readings from various instruments were taken by the Fort William schoolmaster five times a day. Data from the two observatories allowed variations on the vertical physical properties of the atmosphere to be evaluated, and the information gathered added to knowledge of climatic change until both stations were closed in 1904.

Campbell's Waverley Temperance Hotel in Gordon Square, with the bus waiting to depart for North Ballachulish (where it connected with the ferry across Loch Leven). The very modern Highland Regional Council offices now stand on the site of the hotel.

The West End Hotel - as it was in the early part of this century.

Gordon Square, Fort William.

Gordon Square has changed dramatically over the years, and the railway station (left) and MacBrayne's Shipping Office have now both been demolished. The building showing a shop front at the corner of the High Street subsequently became part of the Grand Hotel, and St Mary's Church has been converted to offices. One building, however, remains unchanged; the Highland Hotel looks down from the hillside exactly as it has done for the last century.

The paddle steamer *Fusilier* at Fort William Pier, sometime before 1910. The *Fusilier*, which was based at Oban at this time, mainly worked the summer sea excursion up Loch Linnhe. This was the heyday of rail and steamer travel, which in an age before the motor car provided a better co-ordinated and integrated transport network than is possible to imagine today.

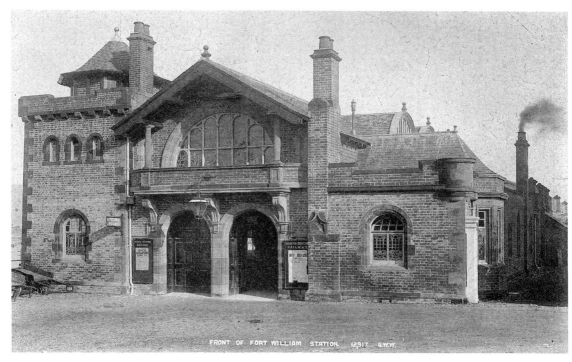

In common with most Victorian public buildings, Fort William railway station was built on a grand scale and intended to last. Completed in 1894, it was a building of which the town could be proud. Interesting stone features were incorporated into the brickwork, and the windows were paned with leaded lights. To the left of the double doorway a poster announces alterations to train timetables for October 1895.

An early photograph of Fort William station from the platform. To take a picture from this perspective today, the photographer would be obliged to stand in the middle of the road which serves as the town by-pass.

THE RAILWAY STATION, FORT WILLIAM.

Hoardings outside the station proclaim famous railway names long gone, including a boast by the North British, North Eastern and Great Northern Railways that their East Coast Route via Berwick and York is 'the shortest and quickest service between Scotland and England'. Fort William Station remained on this site for a little over 80 years. However, during the wholesale redevelopment of the 1970s the buildings were swept away and the station relocated in its present position half a mile away.

A group of postmen pose outside the distinctive facade of Queen Anne Buildings in the High Street, prior to 1900. Macintyre's shop displays postcards for sale. Perhaps someone can confirm whether this was the business of Archibald Macintyre, whose distinctive photographic postcards sold as 'Macintyres Series' until the outbreak of the First World War.

A busy scene taken outside the Macdonald Arms Hotel, looking east along the High Street, sometime in the 1890s. The Caledonian Hotel in Cameron Square can be glimpsed on the right.

The High Street and Palace Hotel (looking west) 1894.

Main Street Fort William, c1930, with some well-to-do tourists and their smart motor cars outside the Palace Hotel. Monzie Square is on the right.

Henry Alexander's Model T Ford, surrounded by an admiring crowd in Cameron Square, 1911. The imposing monument in the background, suitably railed off, was erected in 1852 in memory of local physician Dr. William Kennedy who had died in the previous year. The Square now houses the admirable West Highland Museum which no visitor to Fort William should miss.

A royal occasion! Fort William marks King Edward VII's visit to the town as he makes his way to Mamore Forest Lodge on Loch Leven in 1909.

This memorial to Donald Cameron of Lochiel (1835-1905), XXIV Chief of the Clan, was erected by clansmen and friends in token of their devotion, respect and admiration.

This picture is taken from a stationery postcard advertising the Alexandra Hotel, circa 1900. The hotel appeared on the census listings of 1891 when, with the possible exception of the Lochiel Arms Hotel at Banavie, it was unrivalled for accommodation.

Familiar to several generations of shoppers, this smart branch of the Lochaber Co-operative Society stood at the east end of the High Street, opposite The Parade (for many years the garrison parade ground). The store was demolished in the 1970s to make way for new shops.

The fort which stood on this site for some 240 years was not demolished through battle or siege, but by the coming of the West Highland Railway in 1894, when it was removed to accommodate engine sheds and a locomotive yard. However, the Governor's House was left standing until just before the outbreak of the Second World War. Prior to its demolition the Governor's Room, panelled with Scots pine, was carefully dismantled and re-erected in the West Highland Museum.

Two photographs taken from the same general perspective, looking across the town's waterfront and down Loch Linnhe. The vessel in the upper photograph, manoeuvring towards the pier sometime in the 1880s, seems likely to be the P.S. *Pioneer* . The lower picture can be dated to 1894, and clearly shows the long sea wall constructed to protect the newly built railway track. Positioning the line here proved to be a monumental blunder in town planning as the railway effectively cut Fort William off from the shore. This mistake was not rectified until the mid-1970s.

Following parliamentary assent to the project, Lord Abinger cut the first sod of the West Highland Railway near the Ben Nevis Distillery on the 23rd October 1889. The railway became a reality on August 11th 1894, and was unique in that its complete one hundred mile length was brought into use on a single day. Dignitaries and guests left Glasgow at 8.15 a.m. on a ceremonial train, arriving at a temporary platform near the old fort some 4½ hours later. A large crowd greeted the train's arrival, and pipers played atop a huge battlemented triumphal arch of heather, crowned with flags and the arms of the railway companies. Lochaber rejoiced, and the festivities lasted all day.

Loyal subjects greet King Edward VII as his car crosses Nevis Bridge heading for Mamore, 1909.

The entrance to Glen Nevis lay between two pillars, near the house of the one-time gatekeeper (on the right), beyond General Wade's old military bridge over the River Nevis. The seven mile horse and carriage ride through the picturesque glen made a delightful outing, and was always high on Victorian and Edwardian travellers' itineraries.

A Drive in Glen Nevis

In 1883 gangs of workmen toiled in all weathers to construct a path six feet wide and five miles long from Achintee in Glen Nevis to the top of the Ben. It was accomplished in less than four months at a cost of under £800, and its purpose was to serve the new meteorological observatory then being built on the summit.

Led by a piper, and followed by a crowd of sightseers, soldiers carrying their rifles make their way up the Ben Nevis track in 1897 on an ascent to mark Queen Victoria's Diamond Jubilee. The day was declared a public holiday, and the celebrations concluded with a fireworks display and the lighting of a bonfire on the summit.

Ponies being led up Ben Nevis, 1886. The observatory, built in 1883, was subsequently enlarged by the addition of extra rooms and a thirty foot viewing tower. All the materials for this building work (including lead) were transported up the mountain by Highland ponies. For twenty-one years they regularly provisioned the men stationed on the summit with stores and fuel, although owing to adverse weather conditions journeys were seldom made between the months of November to May.

Tourists such as this party, photographed in 1898, could also make an ascent of the Ben by pony. A toll of 3/- (15p) was collected from those on horseback (1/- for walkers), the fee being payable at the 'Halfway House'. The waters of Loch Linnhe and Loch Eil can be seen over a shoulder of the Ben.

Motor Ascent of Ben Nevis (At the Lake)

MOTOR CAR AT THE OBSERVATORY ON TOP OF BEN NEVIS.

Henry Alexander, last seen in Cameron Square at sea level, makes progress towards the summit of Ben Nevis in his Ford. The ascent was successful, and although made over several days (and with some assistance), was nevertheless a noteworthy achievement. Every stage of Alexander's journey was recorded by the bevy of photographers who followed his progress.

Between 1883 and 1904, this building was home to the meteorologists (a staff superintendent and two assistants) who manned the observatory. At 4406 feet above sea level, weather conditions were often ferocious, making the hourly readings impossible. The external thermometers, gauges and instruments were frequently covered in solid ice, buried in snow, or simply blown away in hurricane force gales of up to 150 mph. Sometimes a powdering of snow even found its way into the living quarters, although this photograph, taken on 30th July 1885, looks serene enough. The station was connected by telegraph cable to Fort William enabling weather reports and other data to be transmitted.

During the often severe weather of the winter months, the station was unable to receive supplies of either fuel or food, so nine months' provisions were usually kept in reserve. Here, the packmen and their ponies, having made a successful delivery, pose for a photograph before making their way down the mountain.

The main purposes of the observatory were to give warning of the approach of south-west storms from the Atlantic, and to investigate vertical gradients of pressure, temperature and humidity in conjunction with the low level station at Achintore. Hourly readings were made, and the lowest temperature recorded was 1.8° F on 7th February 1895. The highest, taken on 24th June 1887, was 67° F. Here, the observer is seen writing up the log in 1885.

From time to time these buildings would be completely snowed in, and in order to reach the instruments during their first winter the observers had to tunnel 30 feet out of the doorway through snowdrifts 12 feet deep. When the viewing tower was added it incorporated an elevated exit from the observatory, making access to the instruments easier. Later enlarged to an 'hotel', the Refreshment Room advertised Bovril in a window by the entrance - very warming, no doubt!

Ben Nevis.   Observatory Hotel.

In 1894 the small temperance hotel could provide sleeping accommodation for over a dozen guests. Tea, bed and breakfast was available for half a guinea (52½p) - a small sum to pay for the proud boast in future years that you had slept on the top of Ben Nevis!

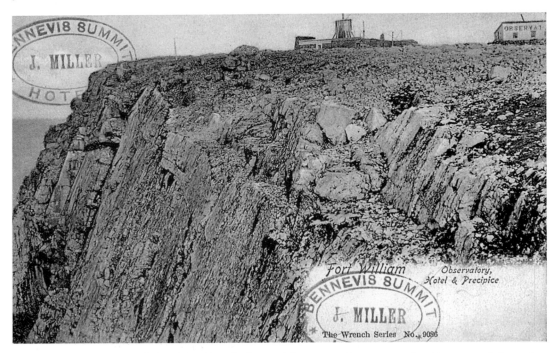

James Miller operated the Hotel and also sold postcards stamped with a special oval cachet in violet ink. These acted as 'proof' of ascent, and the purchasers added messages of which these are typical: 'Greetings from the clouds'; 'I was higher than King, Lords and Commons'; or 'Nearer Heaven than you will ever be'.

ON THE ROOF OF BRITAIN, THE OBSERVATORY RUINS AND INDICATOR
SUMMIT OF BEN NEVIS, FORT WILLIAM.   5166.

The Ben Nevis Observatory was abandoned in 1904 following the inability of the Scottish Meteorological Society and their associates to reach agreement with central government over the level of subsidy required to cover running costs. Present day climbers are often unaware of the history of this remote spot, and seeing the heaps of stone and ruins of walls on the summit, they enquire whether anyone ever lived here. This photograph was taken during the 1950s.

Henry Alexander successfully completed his descent of the mountain in a matter of hours. His feat provided enormous publicity for the Ford Motor Company, and no doubt benefited his father, who operated Edinburgh's main Ford agency. The filming of cars in exotic locations for advertising purposes is apparently not a purely modern phenomenon!

LOCHABER: HERE AND THERE

The 'Rough Bounds' of Knoydart, as the western districts of Lochaber between Loch Hourn and Loch Nevis are known, form a peninsula opposite Skye. Inverie is the sole village in this unparalleled setting, often described as 'Europe's last great wilderness'. From the eastern side only stalkers' tracks over difficult terrain connect with the village, so that of necessity all supplies come by boat from Mallaig. In 1853, three hundred crofters (one third of the Estate) were evicted to Canada to make way for sheep rearing which was seen as more commercially desirable.

Glenquoich Post Office, one of Scotland's more remote post offices, looks tranquil enough in this picture, taken c1910. However, the influx of tourists, fisher-folk and stalkers caused a considerable seasonal increase in the business handled.

In September 1904, King Edward VII spent a week as a stalking guest of Lord and Lady Burton of Dochfour in this large, rambling old house on Loch Quoich. Two great deer drives were organised involving stalkers and gamekeepers drawn from a wide area, but no stags fell to the royal rifle. The event was repeated in 1905. Fifty years later, the damming of Loch Quoich for hydro-electric power resulted in the destruction of the lodge, and now the only indications that a building of some significance once existed are the stunted remnants of the former policies. The picture below shows the drawing room at the Lodge, c1900.

The Tomdoun Hotel overlooks Loch Garry and was built in the 1880s to replace an earlier drovers' inn. It was an important coaching inn owing to its situation at the junction of Telford's road from Invergarry to Kinloch Hourn, and the route which branched northwards to Cluanie Bridge, Glen Shiel and Skye. This latter road was flooded and abandoned when the Loch Loyne hydro scheme raised the level of the loch, although the line of the old road and its crumbling bridges may still be seen in times of drought. When the new section of the A87 was opened in 1961, this formerly important route north of Tomdoun was effectively circumvented.

Captioned 'Highland Hut, Lochaber', this 1890s photograph shows the type of simple stone, turf and thatch structure that was typically home to many in rural Lochaber. A fire in the centre of the floor allowed maximum radiation of heat, the smoke exiting through a central chimney. Weighted ropes (visible in this picture, hanging down the side of the building with rocks attached to them) were used to secure the roof. Life must have been hard for the inhabitants, and in stark contrast to those at the other end of the social spectrum in Victorian Britain.

Before the advent of motor transport, horses were changed at the Invergarrry Hotel, which was an important stop on the road from Fort William to Skye. This picture was taken c1905.

The small obelisk at Invergarry commemorates one of those bloody deeds so frequently found in Highland history - in this case the Keppoch murders of 1663 and the reprisals taken against the seven perpetrators of the crime. Prior to being presented to the Glengarry chief, their severed heads were washed in this spring, which has been known as Tobar nan Ceann (Well of the Heads) ever since.

In May 1746, the house at Achnacarry was razed to the ground by Cumberland's troops as an act of revenge for Lochiel's support for the Stuart cause. The present building, completed in the early 19th century, is the home of Sir Donald H. Cameron of Lochiel, 26th Chief of Clan Cameron whose family has lived here for generations. During the Second World War, Achnacarry was used as a training centre for Commandos. For those interested in clan and regimental history, Jacobite and Commando artefacts, a visit to the Clan Cameron Museum is a must.

Lady Hermonie Cameron laying Foundation Stone, Achnacarry Church.

Achnacarry lies in the parish of Kilmallie, and several alternative sites for the church were considered before this one was chosen. Interestingly enough, neither the minutes of the church trustees nor the foundation stone itself record the date of the ceremony shown. Nevertheless, the Clan museum has a silver trowel used by Lady Hermione Cameron and bearing the date July 1911, thus confirming when the foundation stone was laid. It is thought the church opened for worship in 1913.

The SS *Rifle* lies at anchor on Loch Arkaig, c1890. Built in 1861, she was acquired by the Achnacarry Estate about 1870 and used for transporting stalking parties to and from the wild hills which encircle the loch. At sheep shearing times, she would tow a barge to bring the clippings down from the sheep hirsels (feeding grounds) at the remote head of Loch Arkaig. By the 1930s she was at the end of her working life and was sunk and abandoned, although happily the hull was raised from the loch a few years ago, to be reconstructed and exhibited at the Scottish Maritime Museum in Irvine.

Gairlochy Station, 1914. Over-engineered and over-costly, the twenty-four mile length of the Invergarry and Fort Augustus Railway ran from Spean Bridge to Fort Augustus Pier on Loch Ness. The first train set off to a blast on a gold whistle, but the line, which passed through sparsely populated country, was never profitable. Indeed, the facilities lavished at the hamlet of Gairlochy would not have disgraced Fort William. There were four lines of sidings, loading banks for goods and cattle

(which never materialised), and an unnecessarily large station building which even provided a private waiting room for the proprietors of the nearby Estate. Opened in 1903, and operated intermittently, final closure was dragged out until 1946.

Ring-a-ring of roses at Blarour School, Spean Bridge, c1920.

Spean Bridge Station under construction, 1894, with the contractor's locomotive and wagon at the platform. West Highland Railway station buildings were finished in 'Swiss chalet' style with overhanging roofs (incorporating a storm screen at each end) and exterior walls faced with birch shingles which were imported from Switzerland especially for the purpose.

INVERLOCHY CASTLE AND BEN NEVIS, FORT WILLIAM

During the Second World War Achnacarry became the headquarters of the Commandos and more than 20,000 men were trained in the rugged terrain of Lochaber. In September 1952, H.M. Queen Elizabeth, The Queen Mother, unveiled this striking memorial commemorating their achievements. Situated at the junction of the Gairlochy and main Fort William to Inverness road, the monument, designed by Scott Sutherland, stands nine feet high above its plinth. 'To them danger was a spur, and the unknown but a challenge.'

The opulent Victorian extravaganza which is Inverlochy Castle (once the seat of Lord Abinger and now an hotel of international repute), lies three miles north of Fort William in the shadow of Ben Nevis. Queen Victoria stayed here for a week in 1873 and recorded in her diary that she had never seen a lovelier or more romantic spot. Granted water rights in perpetuity, the Castle has a supply of pure sparkling water from the slopes of Ben Nevis.

A smart turn–out for the photographer on the station platform at Roy Bridge in the early years of this century (the man standing on the extreme right of the group also appears in front of the hotel in the next photograph). Nowadays, this station is unmanned so you will look in vain for a station-master with gold braid on his hat (or indeed, for any staff at all). Even worse, the buildings either side of the track have been demolished.

Victorian and Edwardian travellers found the Roy Bridge Hotel an excellent base for exploring Glen Spean, the Monessie Gorge and, of course, the Parallel Roads of Lochaber. The latter, a spectacular example of deglaciation, can be seen to good effect in Glen Roy where the hillsides are scarred with shelves up to 70 feet wide. These run horizontally around the mountainsides at exactly 1149, 1068 and 857 feet above sea level without variation, and mark the shorelines of huge ice-dammed lakes which once filled the valleys.

Tulloch Station, Glen Spean, c1905. Although the West Highland Railway Station nameboard proclaimed 'Tulloch for Lochlaggan and Kingussie' the latter was thirty-two miles away by road. To facilitate and expand connections along Loch Lagganside, the West Highland Railway partly financed new stabling for the horses at Tulloch.

The Loch Laggan Hotel is about equidistant between Tulloch and Kingussie. Here, the Tulloch coach is about to embark on the remaining seventeen miles of the journey to Kingussie where it connected with the Highland line.

The distant signal gives priority to an as yet unseen Glasgow-bound train making the steep ascent form Glen Spean, while the train for Fort William pauses at Corrour Station, c1910. At 1347 feet above sea level, Corrour is the highest and most remote station on the rail network; indeed the word 'remote' seems quite inadequate to describe it. The line passed over Sir John Stirling Maxwell's 60,000 acre Corrour Estate, and the nearest tarred road to the station was (and still is) eight miles away. Note the snow fences; in these exposed hills, the wind can quickly drift snow to house height.

When this postcard was sold the 'new' lodge at Corrour, overlooking Loch Ossian, had only recently been built. The loch is noted both for its splendid trout and for being (at 1269 feet above sea level) the highest of any size in Scotland. Posted at Corrour on 19th March 1904, the message reads 'The loch is still frozen and has been for nine weeks'. Fire destroyed these substantial buildings in the 1940s, and a new, smaller lodge was subsequently built.

The Nether Lochaber Stores (established 1875) are located between the Corran Ferry and the village of Onich, about nine miles south of Fort William. In this turn of the century photograph, the well-stocked shop displays a fine selection of postcards for sale.

A conveyance for Fort William stands outside Onich Post Office, sometime before the First World War.

Situated at the confluence of Loch Linnhe and Loch Leven, Cuilchenna Village, Onich, enjoys a south facing position with extensive mountain views in all directions. This 1890s photograph was taken by the Oban photographers, McIsaac and Riddle.

The joys of the open road! A car speeds through the village towards North Ballachulish, c1935.

Onich and North Ballachulish are contiguous, and this 1898 photograph shows the road as it sweeps past St. Bride's Church towards the narrows and the ferry crossing point across Loch Leven. The Ballachulish Hotel lies over the water on the extreme right. Note the cultivated strips of rich soil and raised beach deposits (products of the Ice Age when so much of this land lay under huge glaciers).

There was a ferry service across the swirling fast flowing currents between North and South Ballachulish for hundreds of years. However, in Autumn 1975 a bridge was built, the ferries withdrawn, and the frustrating delays of former times passed into history. In this Edwardian scene, the rowers are pulling hard towards the slipway beneath the distant Loch Leven Hotel; anxious moments perhaps for the chauffeur and the travellers seated in the bow. The first car to make a crossing in this way did so in May 1906.

In the 1920s single cars were carried across Loch Leven on a motor boat equipped with a turntable. The Ballachulish Hotel is on the right of this picture.

A huge car headlamp (right foreground) is visible as the ferryman secures the boat at the jetty, having brought a vehicle from South Ballachulish in 1924. Higher up the slipway, below the Loch Leven Hotel, two cars await loading for the return trip across the narrows.

The last visit of His Majesty to the Highlands. Mamore Forest Lodge, Kinlochleven. Jackson's Series. Kinlochleven.

Situated in a large deer forest at the head of Loch Leven, Mamore Lodge has played host to royalty on more than one occasion. Here, King Edward VII is seen departing Mamore on his last visit to the Highlands in 1909. He died in May the following year.

After being culled, deer are hung in venison larders – buildings of some importance on Highland stalking estates. Such larders are found in all sizes and varying types of buildings, but this one at Kinlochmore Lodge (photographed c1910) is a truly enormous example, put into perspective by the two figures standing near the entrance.

At the turn of the 20th century, Kinlochleven consisted of about half a dozen cottages. However, this changed after a 1904 Act of Parliament established the Loch Leven Water and Electric Power Company, which provided a cheap and plentiful local source of electricity. The North British Aluminium Company was already using the benefits of cheap hydro-electric power to smelt aluminium at Foyers, and Kinlochleven followed suit, taking advantage of increasing world demand for the new light metal. Four miles away, above the village on Rannoch Moor, a concrete dam wall 2800 feet long and 85 feet high was constructed to contain the Blackwater Reservoir, which initially provided a water catchment area of 55 square miles. The 1½ mile pipe track (which the Blackwater Falls were redirected through) carried water to the power house, with the reduction factory and carbon electrode plant established alongside it. Building materials were shipped into a newly constructed harbour, and houses built to accommodate the workers. The first metal was produced in Kinlochleven in 1907, and two years later the factory was producing 8000 tons of aluminium each year; about a third of total world output.

Workers' houses and the huge turbine hall (centre) in Kinlochleven, c1908, with continuing peripheral development very much in evidence. The population of this new company town, which was nearly renamed 'Aluminiumville', had risen to over 1200 inhabitants within two years.

'Pug expresses' as they were somewhat grandly named, were the general workhorses for transporting materials around large construction sites. It has not been possible to establish positively whether this picture (c1908) was taken at the official opening ceremony, but plainly a group of visitors is being shown over the new Kinlochleven plant.

The county boundary between Inverness-shire and Argyll divided Kinlochleven, causing administrative disputes on occasions. But no such difficulty existed for the post office; mail was franked 'Kinlochleven, Argyllshire'.

The road through the small settlement of Glencoe, c1900, with the Pap in the background. In the 1930s, a new highway (said to cost £16,000 a mile) was constructed through the glen, bypassing the village. Seen by some as an act of desecration, it aroused much controversy and many darkly hinted at 'the new massacre of Glencoe'.

The Glencoe Hotel, Clachaig , c1902. Although more than 200 years had already elapsed since the tragic events of 1692, the hotel still displayed a notice saying 'No Campbells Served Here' during the late 19th century.

The infamous Glencoe Massacre took place around Carnach in 1692. Space does not permit repetition of the complex circumstances which led to the tragedy, but suffice to say that a detachment of Campbell troops murdered their MacIain hosts (a sept of the MacDonalds) having accepted their hospitality and resided under their roofs for two weeks. The 'Glen of Weeping' sheds tears not only for the treacherous killing of forty MacIains in their beds, but equally for this deliberate and callous violation of the sacred code of Highland hospitality.

Excursions into Glencoe were always much in demand by tourists. Here, a packed coach makes a stop at Loch Treachtan in 1898.

An upbringing in this desolate and formidable glen with its grim associations must have made a powerful impact on the minds of these young children, c1905. Kingshouse Hotel, a well-known hostelry, lies on the extremity of Lochaber. From here, our journey through Lochaber doubles back along the road to Ballachulish on Loch Leven.

East Laroch Quarry, Ballachulish.

RELIABLE SERIES

Slate Cutting, Ballachulish Quarries.

RELIABLE SERIES

In the second half of the 18th century, slate was being quarried on a small scale at Laroch farm, although by the end of Queen Victoria's reign quarrying was big business in Ballachulish, employing some 400 men. The quarry face was 1400 yards long, and a narrow gauge railway brought the rock to a yard adjoining the railway station by the side of Loch Linnhe. Here, workmen split and trimmed it for roofing slates, as seen in these photographs c1904. The finished supplies were taken away by sea. Slate no longer pays the wages in Ballachulish, and after the quarry closed (c1955) the scars on the hillside above the village were landscaped, disguising the visible reminders of the industry.

The 28 mile Ballachulish branch line from Connel to Loch Leven wound its way up the coast of Benderloch and Appin amid vistas of stunning beauty before terminating at the station named 'Ballachulish (Glencoe) for Kinlochleven', almost under the quarry face. Scenes of industrialisation, heaps of spoil and sounds of rock blasting greeted travellers, providing a stark contrast to what they had just experienced! The line, which had opened in 1903, finally closed in 1966 due to a steady decline in traffic.

Ballachulish Town Hall, c1905. Today, little has changed outwardly, although the cottage on the right has been replaced by modern housing. The former town hall is now used as the Joint Services Mountain Training Centre, and volunteers from the armed services attend courses on rock climbing, hill walking, snow and ice mountaineering and navigation there.

The Ballachulish Hotel, previously glimpsed from the northern shore of Loch Leven (p43), was of particular strategic importance, being situated where narrows provided a short connecting sea link with the north/south land route to Fort William and the Great Glen. The present building dates from Victorian times, but there has been an inn here for centuries. In this 1890s photograph several coaches which used the Glencoe and Appin routes stand near the jetty were the ferry boat is beached. The SS *Fusilier* from Oban made a regular call at the nearby pier. Later still, in 1903, Ballachulish Ferry Station was built a short distance behind the hotel, thus providing a rail connection with the Callander and Oban line at Connel. The combined facilities provided a perfect coming together of services for the Victorian and Edwardian traveller.

A full coach bound for Glencoe waits outside the Ballachulish Hotel c1904. This is one of a series of postcards advertising Glencoe and Glen Etive Coaching Tours.

The mountains of Ardgour, seen across Loch Linnhe, form the background for this 1935 picture. The PS *Iona* is at the pierhead just beyond Kentallen railway station. Since this picture was taken the station has been skilfully converted to the Holly Tree Hotel and Restaurant.

Cuil Bay, Duror. The constituents of this photograph make a pleasant scene: a ploughman with his pair of horses, followed by a host of gulls, and set against the backdrop of the sunlit waters of Loch Linnhe.

THE ROAD TO ARDNAMURCHAN

On the far shore at Corran a lighthouse guards the crossing over the channel between Inverness-shire and Argyll, where Loch Linnhe shrinks to a width of 200 yards. Across the water lie the beautiful but sparsely populated districts of Ardgour, Morvern and Ardnamurchan - a very remote area which was relatively unknown and inaccessible to the traveller of 1892 when this photograph was taken. The Ardgour Hotel and its landing pier are on the right of the far shore, across the loch from the Nether Lochaber Hotel (left foreground).

In 1935 the ferry was upgraded to transport vehicles thus obviating a time-consuming but, it has to be admitted, delightful detour of 45 miles via Kinlocheil to reach the opposite shore at Ardgour.

Corran Lighthouse, built in 1860, was manned until automation in 1970. The vessel in
the foreground is HMS *Victorious*.

Having landed at Ardgour, travellers often felt (and to an extent still do) that they were in a very different
country, 'like some lonely explorer viewing untracked territory' as one wrote in 1949. However, as well as
the hotel there was a general store and a separate post office, which perhaps reassured the visitor
somewhat.

Post Office, Corran, Ardgour.

Ardnamurchan Point, our final destination in this part of the book, lies fifty miles to the west of Ardgour over narrow roads.

In the 1930s the width of the single track road along Sallachan Bay only just accommodated the motor car. Passing places were relatively few and far between, but fortunately at the time traffic was light in this large and remote area. In the last thirty years, enormous improvements have been made to roads such as these. Many narrow, tortuous lengths and loops of abandoned tarmac, indicating a former road, can be seen between Sallachan and Strontian. These are gradually becoming overgrown and merging back into the surrounding moorland, and present day tourists find it difficult to believe that motorists of another era actually drove on them.

Lochaline lies on the Sound, opposite the island of Mull, and in former days was more accessible by sea than by the adventurous road through Morvern. In this 1930s picture, the *Lochinvar* is at the pierhead. She spent almost the whole of her working life on the Oban - Sound of Mull - Tobermory service. Carrying passengers, mail and cargo all the year round, she was an absolutely essential lifeline for the area.

Strontian, at the head of Loch Sunart, 1897. The hotel can be seen on the right.

By the early 18th century, mines in the hills north of Strontian were producing lead, mica and felspar. However, far more significant was the discovery of strontianite in 1764. This subsequently led to the identification of strontium, a metallic element which is present in radioactive fall-out from atomic explosions, and known to us today as strontium 90. The mines have long since closed, but what lingering fame for this little settlement on Loch Sunart!

Surrounded by glorious West Highland scenery, Acharacle is a scattered township at the western end of Loch Shiel. In this turn of the century picture, an unmetalled road leading to Kinlochmoidart curves around the Loch Shiel Hotel, a favourite haunt of fisherfolk.

Having parked their cars, several people wait on the pierhead behind the Loch Shiel Hotel. Trips up and down the eighteen mile length of the loch to Glenfinnan were popular, and guests bound for the hotel would often travel on the West Highland Railway to Glenfinnan and make the remaining stage of their journey by boat down the loch, usually accompanied by the mails for the district. Improved roads resulted in the cessation of the Loch Shiel sailings in September 1967.

The pier, Acharacle, Loch Shiel.

Shielbridge, Acharacle, 1897. David MacBrayne (of shipping fame) acquired this fishing inn on Loch Shiel, adding the annexe on the left in the 1890s. This was not built from scratch, but constructed from a redundant corrugated iron church that MacBrayne bought in Glasgow and had transported to Acharacle, where the sections were re-assembled (minus the spire). Mr C.D. Rudd subsequently purchased the estate, removing the annexe and building a new lodge in its place. However, following 'house warming celebrations' on the 24th March 1900, a fire started in the original building. This raged for three days and spread to the newly built lodge which was completely destroyed, although Mr Rudd recommenced building on the site again immediately.

This photograph (c1904) shows Shielbridge House as rebuilt by Mr Rudd. Of the two neighbouring properties it was his preferred residence, although it was demolished in 1951 (under different ownership), reputedly for reasons of high taxation.

Mr Rudd's 1903 Panhard-Levassor at the entrance to Shielbridge, 1905. At the beginning of the 20th century motor cars were unusual, and quite a talking point in remote country districts. This car was thought to be still in use in Fort William until the outbreak of the Second World War. (Photograph reproduced here by kind permission of Susan Girling).

Charles Dunell Rudd (1844-1916) went to South Africa in 1865 and ultimately made his fortune, although not before experiencing more than his fair share of setbacks and hardship. He was a friend and business partner of Cecil Rhodes, after whom Rhodesia was named, and together they co-founded a number of companies including De Beers Mining Co. Ltd. In 1902 Rudd, by that time a wealthy diamond magnate, retired to Scotland having acquired the huge Ardnamurchan Estate (embracing virtually the whole peninsula) six years earlier. At the turn of the century, Rudd not only rebuilt his property at Shielbridge after it was gutted by fire, but also had a 'Scottish Baronial' castle under construction at Glenborrodale. The castle overlooked Loch Sunart and lay eight miles away 'over the hill' from Shielbridge. (Photograph reproduced here by kind permission of Susan Girling).

SALEN-HOTEL

In the early years of the century, the Salen Hotel was the only licensed public house in this area, enjoying a monopoly which the Loch Shiel Hotel at Acharacle was unable to challenge. It made several applications for a licence, although these were repeatedly opposed. The Salen Hotel is situated at a meeting of roads, and this 1930s picture shows the former B850 route on the right. This led to Acharacle and ultimately ended at the small pier at Kinlochmoidart. Travelling downhill and passing to the left of the hotel, the B8007 wound around the shores of Loch Sunart before eventually reaching Kilchoan and, five miles further on, Ardnamurchan Point.

Market day. Salen, Loch Sunart, c1904.

The view across the head of Salen Bay, taken in the 1930s. The prominent building on the hillside was the Duncraig Hotel.

Many proprietors of large estates in Scotland considered the ownership of a steam yacht to be almost mandatory. Mr. Rudd's yacht *Mingary* was built by the Ailsa Shipbuilding Company of Troon in 1898 and bore the name of an ancient castle on his estate near Kilchoan. The captain of this magnificent vessel, Dan McKinnon from Kylerhea in Skye, lived at the anchorage in Salen Bay. *Mingary* was a familiar sight up and down the coast, especially at Oban, but travelled much more widely. A cruise to the Mediterranean required a full complement of 21 crew members, and it was said that her annual running costs amounted to more than the total expenses for the whole Ardnamurchan estate! (Photograph reproduced here by kind permission of Susan Girling).

The MV *Lochshiel* was a cargo ship with a capacity of about 200 tons, seen here discharging a mixed cargo at Salen Pier sometime in the 1930s. In an area of generally poor roads, the natural lanes of communication were by sea, and the *Lochshiel*'s relatively small size made her ideally suited to this type of work.

A backward glance towards the peak of Ben Resipol (2775 feet). This photograph illustrates the nature of the road to Ardnamurchan, which winds along the northern shore of Loch Sunart through oak and birch woods, past banks hanging with ferns, and alongside beautiful bays. Over the last thirty years I have developed a particular affection for this gem of a road. However, until the improvements of recent years, blind summits were not uncommon and there were comparatively few passing places on its single track.

Laga Bay, Loch Sunart. From the 1830s, the Highland Clearances resulted in the steady decline of Ardnamurchan's population, and in 1853 eight tenants in Laga were evicted to make way for a sheep farm. One of the largest gatherings in the area took place in August 1903 when Mr Rudd's daughter married Sir Eldon Gorst. To celebrate the wedding, a fete was prepared on the picturesque Strath of Laga and 800 guests were entertained.

Charles Rudd decided to build a property fit for the Laird of Ardnamurchan on his newly purchased estate, and Glenborrodale Castle rose on the site of a mansion house that had been erected by the previous owner. (The coach house and stables behind the site, reputedly 300 years old and thus the oldest buildings in the locality, were retained intact). Mr Donald Fletcher, a well known contractor from Tobermory, was engaged to undertake the building work, and labour was drawn both from the immediate area and from Mull and Skye. A wage of £1 or 25/- (£1.25) was paid for a six day week, depending on skills. Puffers (small cargo boats) brought red sandstone from Annan in Dumfriesshire into Glenborrodale Bay, just below the elevated building site, and the building was completed in three years. Cecil Rhodes himself attended the occasion of the house warming which was held in August 1901.

The approach to Kilchoan. Where the long arm of Loch Sunart broadens out into the Sound, the village looks directly across to the island of Mull. Getting here from Acharacle by road in the 1940s was not without difficulty, as Arthur Gardner described in his book *Western Highlands*: 'The public mail-car, by which we travelled, was an ancient contraption which did the twenty miles or so in under four hours! Each time we came to a hill we thought we should never reach the top, but in spite of its rattles and groans and roars, it triumphantly breasted each rise, and brought us to our destination!'

Until the late 1890s, mail and cargo steamers delivered an average of 4 tons of cargo to Kilchoan Bay each week. Vessels were met by the local ferry boat, into which the goods and passengers were transferred before being rowed ashore. The ferry operator levied a fee of 3d for each passenger and parcel conveyed this way. When Mingary pier was built in 1898 at a cost of £2,000 these arrangements were no longer necessary, although the MacBrayne boats showed some initial reluctance to use the pier.

Kilchoan, set on its picturesque bay, seen from Ormsaig. The peak of Ben Hiant which dominates western Ardnamurchan at 1729 feet is on the right.

When this picture was taken around 1900, Achnaha, on the lonely road to Sanna Bay, must surely have been one of the neatest crofting townships imaginable. Until the spring of 1925 the road ended here. However, largely due to the campaigning efforts of a certain Miss Donaldson it was then extended by a further two miles to Sanna.

FORDS OVER BURN AT OCKLE. M.E.M.D.

There were many tiny settlements along the rugged northern coast of Ardnamurchan, and ruined crofts and heaps of stone are eloquent reminders of the Highland Clearances and the desolation they left behind. This is the small hamlet of Ockle, c1920. (Photograph by M.E.M. Donaldson).

RUM AND EIGG FROM ACHATENY, ARDNAMURCHAN

Achateny not only has a gloriously sandy beach at Port Bàn , but also enjoys superb views towards the islands of Eigg and Rum, which form the background to this photograph.

Lower Sanna c1930.

Miss M.E.M. Donaldson fell under the spell of Ardnamurchan in the early years of this century, and in particular with the magnificent shell sand beach at Sanna with its seashore tracks, abundance of interesting flora, and cattle by the shore. Overlooking this bay on which Atlantic rollers break, she resolved to build a house that would be entirely in harmony with the environment, using traditional stone and heather thatch. By 1927, her dream had been realised. Writing from Sanna Bheag, she produced a number of carefully researched books on the history and traditions of the Western Highlands and Islands. She was also an accomplished photographer, frequently to be seen on location with the heavy, cumbersome equipment of the period in tow. (Photograph by M.E.M. Donaldson).

Puffers were ideal for delivering bulky cargoes (in this case coal) directly to the beach. Some of the materials for Miss Donaldson's house arrived from Mull in this way, to be unloaded at low tide and transported the remaining few yards to the building site by horse and cart . (Photograph by M.E.M. Donaldson).

COAL "PUFFER" IN AT SANNA BHEAG, MUCK & RUM IN DISTANCE.   M.E.M.D.

Ardnamurchan Lighthouse has the distinction of being located on Britain's most westerly mainland point, and is consequently prominently marked on Admiralty charts and instantly recognised by mariners. The tower, which is 114 feet high and constructed of Mull granite, was completed in the middle of the last century. A flight of 140 steps around the hollow core gives access to the lamp room and provides spectacular views over the Inner and Outer Hebrides. Sadly, the resident keepers were withdrawn in August 1988. Now, as dusk falls over Ardnamurchan, an automatic signal is transmitted to this lonely station from the Northern Lighthouse Board in Edinburgh activating the light which has shone out since 1849. While outwardly nothing has changed, there is now one important difference - nobody is at home.

THE ROAD TO THE ISLES

The modern 'Road to the Isles' (the A830) is a fine carriageway for much of its 48 mile length to Mallaig, although it was not always so. One hundred years ago the road reached only as far as Arisaig, and this romantic but none too fanciful picture would be instantly recognisable to travellers of that era. Even as late as the 1940s, the road was in such an appalling state that garage proprietors in Fort William were guaranteed

a regular source of income from repairing damaged vehicles. The extension of the West Highland Railway to Mallaig at the turn of the century resulted in both road and 'iron road' running within sight of each other for most of their journey; we will follow the course of both.

In 1895 the West Highland Railway Company built a short spur from Fort William to Banavie where a new station lay alongside, but some distance below the bank of the Caledonian Canal. The intention was to attract a portion of the considerable passenger and freight traffic plying the Caledonian Canal to and from Inverness. In this picture, the train stands at the landing stage on the canal, and embarkation is almost complete as the SS *Gondolier* makes ready to depart, c1903. (Passengers reached the landing stage by walking up the embankment from the station below; freight wagons had to be shunted up a steep gradient of 1 in 24).

A rare photograph of rolling stock on the move taken from the platform of Banavie Pier station, c1914.

Banavie station looking east, c1914 (not to be confused with the Pier station which lay half a mile away). Opened in 1901, this was the first stop on the newly constructed Fort William to Mallaig section of track. You will look in vain for the building today; having become unstaffed, it suffered severely from vandalism and was subsequently demolished.

A flight of eight locks marks the southern end of the Caledonian Canal at its entrance to Loch Linnhe. This remarkable engineering achievement, the work of Thomas Telford, has always been known as Neptune's Staircase. Each lock consists of a drop of eight feet of water, so that a vessel entering the chain changes its level sixty-four feet before it resumes sailing in open water.

To the extreme discomfort of the Highland waiter, an American made himself obnoxious by his contemptuous remarks on the scenery. Nothing could compare with the vastness and grandeur of the landscape back home; Loch Lomond, for example, was a 'puddle', and Ben Nevis a mere 'wart'. At length the exasperated waiter procured a live lobster which he secreted in the American's bed. Hardly had the tourist gone to sleep than the lobster caught him by the toe with a grasp like a vice. The next morning he readily conceded that although the scenery might not compare to that in the States, Scottish fleas were the biggest he had ever experienced! The 'Banavie flea' joke had long passed into history when this photograph of the Lochiel Arms Hotel was taken, c1895.

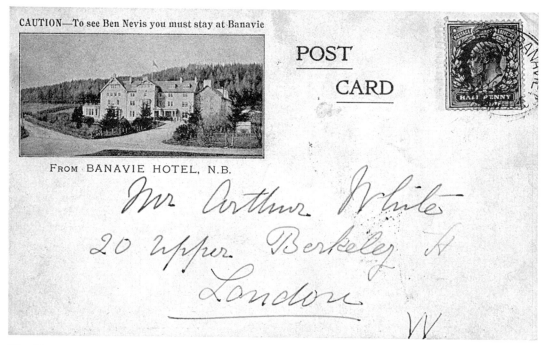

CAUTION—To see Ben Nevis you must stay at Banavie

POST
CARD

HALF PENNY

FROM BANAVIE HOTEL, N.B.

*Mr Arthur White
20 Upper Berkeley St
London
W*

The Banavie Hotel (Lochiel Arms Hotel) was always busy with 'one-nighters' sailing up from Oban in the afternoon, dining and sleeping, and sailing on to Inverness via the Caledonian Canal the following morning. The claim in the hotel publicity material (as on this postcard of 1903), that Ben Nevis could be best seen from Banavie - and not at all from Fort William - brought it into conflict with the latter's town council. The hotel subsequently suffered a disastrous fire, and the ruins could still be seen in the 1930s.

Corpach Pier, dwarfed by the bulk of Ben Nevis. The coaches on the quayside provided a link with the Caledonian Canal at Banavie where travellers could continue their journey to Inverness.

Corpach canal basin (photographed in 1898) marks the southern end of the Caledonian Canal, and gives access to Loch Linnhe and the Atlantic. Sixty miles away at Inverness the canal enters the Moray Firth and the North Sea. On the extreme right of this photograph, a newly made track runs behind the terraced houses overlooking the lock-gates. Just beyond these houses, a large area is being cleared for Corpach railway station, which opened in 1901.

Fort William photographed from across Loch Linnhe, with Corpach in the foreground. The large white building was the immediate predecessor to the present day Corpach Hotel.

The Corpach Hotel - a well-known staging post on the Road to the Isles - photographed in the 1890s.

Four days after raising his standard at Glenfinnan, Prince Charles Edward Stuart and his followers reached Fassiefern, the home of Lochiel's brother John. It was here that Prince Charlie was informed of the opposing Hanoverian army's march from Stirling under Sir John Cope. Tradition has it that whilst at Fassiefern the Prince picked a white rose from the garden which later became the White Cockade emblem of the '45.

Flowers bloom on the platform at Locheilside station. This building has suffered the same fate as some others along the route, where a tubular 'bus shelter' has replaced the original and distinctive West Highland Railway structure.

Set in an amphitheatre of mountains at the head of Loch Shiel's 'endless' expanse, Glenfinnan's setting is truly grand. Prince Charlie's monument, crowned with the figure of a kilted Highlander, is the focus of Jacobite sympathy and sentiment. Each year, about 25,000 tourists buy tickets at the National Trust for Scotland's Visitor Centre nearby, and thousands more admire this view from the elevated position of the railway, or as they pass by along the Road to the Isles.

Contrary to popular belief, this tower is unlikely to mark the very spot where the white, blue and red standard was unfurled in 1745 to call out the Clans. Authorities are now generally agreed that a low knoll, about a quarter of a mile north-west of the visitor centre is the more likely location. However, technicalities aside, the train of events set in motion here was certainly

momentous. The Jacobite army reached as far south as Derby, just 120 miles from London, causing great consternation in the capital. This monument, which commemorates all the loyal clansmen who gave their lives in support of Prince Charlie, represents a tragic echo of a lost cause which ended at Culloden.

The *Clanranald* (seen here landing passengers at Glenfinnan, c1905) provided a service to Acharacle at the far distant end of Loch Shiel six days a week. This view across the marshy margins at the head of the loch shows the church of St. Mary and St. Finan, which has such a tranquil atmosphere in this land of stirring events. In the background, the scars of the newly completed railway are visible on the hillside.

'A thing so delicate that the fairies might have built it', the Glenfinnan viaduct was Robert McAlpine's crowning achievement on a railway line that incorporated so many notable features. The curved structure is 100 feet high and 416 yards in length, and consists of 21 arched spans of 50 feet each. McAlpine was known in engineering circles as 'Concrete Bob' for his use of mass concrete, then a relatively new

medium, and this was the first concrete viaduct to be built in Britain. It is said that during construction a horse and cart fell into one of the viaduct's piers and remain entombed there to this day.

In this pre-Second World War photograph, a number of passengers wait on the station platform at Glenfinnan for a Fort William bound train. That this important station has survived intact is due to the dedication and enthusiasm of John Barnes and a small band of like-minded volunteers. Eight years of hard work have ensured the survival of a complete working station, which also houses a museum and shop. A number of other attractions are reaching fruition, and rail enthusiasts or voluntary helpers who wish to support the excellent work of The Glenfinnan Station Museum Trust should contact Mr Barnes, who will be delighted to hear from them!

The McKellaig, Cairn, Glenfinnan.

The Stage House Inn lies equidistant between Fort William and Arisaig, and as its name implies horses were changed here at one time. In 1900, as the West Highland Railway was under construction, Donald MacKellaig moved here from Arisaig to take over the inn. He ran it until his death ten years later, when his son took over until 1938. It was a well-known fishing hotel and a brochure for that year states the total catch: 11 salmon 110½ pounds; 789 sea-trout 1274¼lbs; 25 brown trout 23¼lbs; 125 finnocks 74½lbs. The newly opened railway station is visible high on the hillside in the top right of this photograph, c1905.

This cairn, bearing the inscription *In memory of Donald MacKellaig, Stage House Inn, 28th November 1910. Sith dhia dha.*, stands on a loop of the old road. As was the custom Mr MacKellaig, a well-respected member of the local community, was laid to rest on Eilean Fhionain, a traditional burying ground in Loch Shiel.

From Glenfinnan the road drops steeply towards Loch Eilt, famous both for its trout and the distinctive small islets on which Scots firs grow.

It is difficult to imagine that 2000 navvies - tunnellers, horse-handlers, pick and shovel men - were camped at Kinlochailort during the construction of the railway. There are three buildings of significance in this photograph (c1903), all of which have disappeared in the last ten years. From left to right they are the inn with its three gables (destroyed by fire), the signal box, and the station (both demolished).

Kinlochailort Inn, 1896. At the end of the 19th century, this famous inn and staging post was an old-fashioned building, with panelled passages perfumed with the reek of peat-fires. Passing tinkers who could neither read nor write would bring their unopened letters here so that the landlady could read them aloud.

Inverailort House lies a short distance from the inn on the new road to Kinlochmoidart (constructed in 1966). Parts of the building date back to the middle of the 18th century. During the Second World War Inverailort was one of several 'Arisaig Schools' where Commandos were trained by Colonel David Stirling of the SAS. At the time the whole area was a restricted zone, closed to all but permit holders.

A successful day on the hill, sometime before the First World War.

At this point the road to Mallaig drops to sea-level, and having passed beneath the viaduct sweeps around the rugged shore of Loch nan Uamh. Passing beneath this arch can be likened to parting a curtain or opening a door as it reveals the view of Loch nan Uamh, a jumble of rock and water bordered with craggy wooded hillsides; a view which bursts upon the traveller with a breath-taking force that never palls. For Prince Charles Edward Stuart two hundred and fifty years ago, this loch had special significance . . .

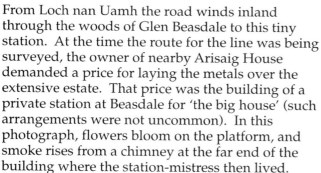

From Loch nan Uamh the road winds inland through the woods of Glen Beasdale to this tiny station. At the time the route for the line was being surveyed, the owner of nearby Arisaig House demanded a price for laying the metals over the extensive estate. That price was the building of a private station at Beasdale for 'the big house' (such arrangements were not uncommon). In this photograph, flowers bloom on the platform, and smoke rises from a chimney at the far end of the building where the station-mistress then lived.

Miss Mary Campbell, photographed on the platform at Beasdale station c1922. As station-mistress she occupied accommodation within the station buildings from 1901 until her retirement in 1927. Remembered as a good gardener, she plainly used her talents to good effect around her domain. Note the letters NBR on her hat; the North British Railway worked this line until 1923. (Photograph reproduced here by kind permission of Ruth and John Smither).

Towards the end of July 1745, the *Du Teillay* entered Loch nan Uamh (Loch of the Caves) to put Prince Charles Edward Stuart ashore, accompanied by a handful of followers. The white sands just below Borrodale House where they landed are still known as the 'Prince's Beach'. Borrodale was the farmhouse of Angus Macdonald, tenant of Clanranald, and it was here in a room at the western end of the building (on the left of the picture) that the Prince held court with clansmen for several days, seeking support for his cause. After the rout at Culloden a year later, he was here again, hotly pursued as a fugitive and with a price on his head. However, Hanoverian troops under Captain Ferguson had already put Borrodale House to the flames, and on the 20th September 1746 *L'Hereux* bore the exiled Prince away from Loch nan Uamh and Scotland. The sad venture was over and he was never to return.

Arisaig House (south elevation), c1910. At the tender age of three months, F.D.P. Astley inherited considerable family wealth derived from Cheshire coal and iron industries, and during his mid-twenties purchased the extensive Arisaig Estate. The architect Philip Webb was commissioned to design a mansion house appropriate to such responsibilities. Using prodigious amounts of stone the house, terraces and walled gardens, deer larders and gardeners' bothy were built

for £12,000 - and that figure included adjacent cottages and farm buildings! Unfortunately, Astley did not live to enjoy his property for long, dying in 1868 just four years after the house was completed.

In 1935 Major Jack Courtauld and his family took Arisaig House for the stalking season, as was their custom. A visitor to the house at that time recounted to me in 1988 the dramatic events of the 6th and 7th of September 1935. Shortly after midnight, a fire was found to have taken hold behind a beam in one of the servants' bedrooms on the top floor. Everyone was roused and immediately evacuated to the lawn. However, the roof void was well alight and guests spent the night watching helplessly as the inferno spread. About 9 a.m., the fire brigade arrived from Fort William, although by that time the interior had been entirely gutted and the fire had

burnt itself out. This photograph, taken from the main drive in the immediate aftermath of the fire, shows the ruins of the original 'big house' of Arisaig. (Photograph reproduced here by kind permission of Mr and Mrs E.D. MacMillan).

Arisaig House, c1939. Although adequate insurance cover enabled the house to be rebuilt, normality did not return for long and the property was requisitioned for the duration of the Second World War. It was initially used by Military Intelligence (Research) and subsequently, from November 1940, by the Special Operations Executive in response to Winston Churchill's call to 'set Europe alight'. Agents destined to be dropped behind enemy lines were trained here in many skills, among them sabotage, subversion and silent killing. For training exercises, the LMS Railway provided redundant track, rolling stock and engines which were blown up behind the house. No such drama today, however! Mr and Mrs John Smither and their family aim to provide peace and quiet for their guests at this Relais and Chateaux hotel.

A scattering of houses around the head of Loch nan Ceall. St. Mary's Church and the Arisaig Hotel are on the extreme left, c1902.

Until the late 1890s the Road to the Isles ended at this hotel, a stone's throw away from the harbour at Arisaig. The forty mile journey from Fort William (via the staging posts at Corpach, Glenfinnan and Lochailort) took seven and a half hours by horse drawn coach - if all went well. The inner reaches of the loch are rocky and require careful navigation, but Arisaig also has the benefit of deeper water nearby at Rhu jetty, which was

once a calling place for MacBrayne boats. Consequently, access could be gained to an enviable network of tours and excursions serving a variety of mainland and island destinations. The extension of 'The Road' northwards by a further eight miles to Mallaig, coupled with the arrival of the West Highland Railway in 1901, resulted in the relative decline in importance of Arisaig.

RHUM FROM BACK OF KEPPOCH

Back of Keppoch lies over the hill from Arisaig and offers panoramic views towards the islands; in this case the peaks of Rum with part of Eigg to the left. The eight miles of sea between mainland and islands can assume every subtle shade between leaden and cobalt - or, as the sun goes down, from polished silver to scarlet.

In the far distance, over the waters of the Sound of Sleat, Skye and the Cuillin ridge make a grand view from Back of Keppoch.

Bracora, 1896. Loch Morar is the deepest freshwater loch in Britain by far, with a depth of more than 1000 feet at the centre. Like Loch Ness it is reputed to have a monster - in this case named Morag.

Morar, c1902. The two most important buildings in the village at this time - the railway station and the hotel - lie either side of 'The Road'. The famous silver sands of Morar are in the bay below.

Before the arrival of the railhead and harbour at the turn of the century, Mallaig was almost unknown, consisting of little more than a handful of black houses facing Skye across the Sound of Sleat. However, within a few short years, the small fishing/crofting settlement laid out by Lord Lovat at the time of the potato famine was transformed into a thriving harbour for fishing fleets. Mallaig became noteworthy as a port of call for island steamers, and increasingly appeared on the itineraries of curious tourists.

Around the turn of the century, the herring industry was still an extremely important force in Mallaig's economy, despite considerable fluctuations in the catch. Indeed, the very reason for bringing the railway to Mallaig at all had been to exploit the resources of the Minch fisheries. By the early 1930s, building development had spilled right across the Point, and there was a semi-permanent smoke haze over the

port from the fifteen kippering sheds then in operation. In the background, the long shape of Eigg resembles a ship riding at anchor, while the mountains of Rum dominate the view to the right.

From Glasnacardoch the route of the railway follows the shore. The road, however, winds up and over a steep hill to make a final descent into Mallaig between the newly built Station Hotel (right) and a group of railway cottages, before reaching an equally new harbour. However, at the conclusion of the journey from Fort William both road and railway terminate within a few yards of each other. The enduring image of this early picture is that of a large building site.

A postcard advertisement for the Station Hotel, postmarked 30th July 1912. After a serious fire in the 1920s, a new building rose on the site as the West Highland Hotel. Its elevated position, looking westwards towards the islands, makes sunsets a speciality here. Evening dinner can suffer disruption as diners slip away between courses to capture on film the last rays of the dying sun as it sets behind Rum, highlighting the mountain tops in a magnificent riot of colour.

THE CENTRE OF WEST HIGHLAND TOURS

Magnificent situation at terminus of West Highland Line.

Deep Sea Fishing, Boating, and Bathing.

Steamer Sailings.

Bracing Climate.

First-class Hotel with every comfort.

Electric Light.

Motor Garage.

Officially appointed to the S.A.C. and A.A.

'En pension' terms.

All particulars on application to the Manager.

STATION HOTEL, MALLAIG
— INVERNESS-SHIRE —

Overlooking the islands of Canna, Rum, Eigg and Muck, Mallaig signal box (photographed in 1901) possibly had the finest view of any on the whole rail network.

Mallaig station in the early days, when the railway line curved around the terminus and ran onto the fish wharf - a hive of activity where for some years the catch would be loaded into special fish vans for despatch by rail. The station canopy (obscured by smoke in this picture) and high retaining wall have only been removed in the last twenty years. Now that the Road to the Isles has been re-routed along the shore it ends close to the station booking office.

HERRING CURING, MALLAIG.   85201.J.V.

Revered as 'the silver darlings', the herring were migratory, and boats and the itinerant fisher-lassies would follow the shoals. The fish arrived off the Hebrides in late May, and experienced girls could gut and grade 60 herring a minute. If there was a glut of fish, their working day might start at 6 a.m. and last until 10 p.m. Seasonally, they lived in 'Chinatown', a local name for an area of wooden huts between the railway and the sea.

Right: Catches of white fish in the quantities displayed in these two photographs (c1905) are unlikely to be seen in Mallaig again. Like other ports around our coasts, Mallaig has suffered fluctuating fortunes due to dwindling fish stocks, and in more recent years a surfeit of E.U. legislation. But although catches have declined Mallaig is still a major fishing port, even though the great days have gone. Today, there is a ready market for shellfish, and the town is attracting increased funding. It also has important connections with the Inner and Outer Hebrides, and the recently introduced roll-on/roll-off facilities have greatly enhanced the ferry connection with Armadale on Skye.

EPILOGUE

It would be remiss, having taken the Road to the Isles, not to say a word or two about the islands that are its destination as they were at the end of Queen Victoria's reign.

Canna, Rum, Eigg and Muck are a strange group of islands, the nearest of which lies eight miles south-west from the Point of Sleat on Skye. Collectively, these Hebridean jewels form the parish of the Small Isles, and although they share much common history with the Western Highlands, they each have very differing characteristics.

Robert Thompson, an international arms dealer and a foreign correspondent for *The Times*, purchased Eigg and Muck in the 1890s. Eigg is a kidney-shaped island (five miles by three), and its spectacular natural feature is a bastion of pitchstone lava rising 1289 feet above sea-level, known as the Sgurr of Eigg, a weird landmark instantly recognisable from all directions. Low lying Muck is much smaller. Both islands prospered under Thompson's proprietorship, with crofting and dairying the principal occupations.

Canna was purchased in 1881 by one Robert Thom, who had generated his wealth from South American trade. He and his son farmed the island and were popular landlords, improving tenants' houses, building the pier and planting trees.

Rum is a mountainous, diamond shaped island, and at eight miles across each axis, the largest of the quartet. The mountains rise abruptly from the sea, and the highest peak is Askival (2663 feet). In 1891, at the age of twenty-two, George Bullough inherited Rum, together with considerable wealth which he lavished on the island. In 1899, Kinloch House was demolished to make way for an ornate, turreted castle, built of red Arran sandstone. It was extravagantly furnished in the manner of the Victorian period. The installation of electricity, under-floor ventilation to clear cigar smoke from the billiard room, a fully sprung ballroom dance floor and an early system of double glazing were all 'firsts' in the islands. Externally he added great glasshouses and conservatories to grow peaches and grapes, and there were even heated pools for exotic reptiles! Everything was on an heroic scale, and about 90 staff were employed in 1901. However, it was not destined to last. The Great War of 1914 brought irreversible changes, and as on many Highland estates the brilliance began to fade. Sir George died in France in 1939. Lady Monica, aged ninety-eight, died in London in 1967. Her coffin was transported by rail to Mallaig, and taken across the Sound to Rum to her final resting place beside her husband in a magnificent Doric mausoleum overlooking the lonely shore at Harris Bay. For Rum, it was the end of an era.

The Bullough Mausoleum, Isle of Rum.